The Five First Saturdays
and Reparation
to the Immaculate Heart
of Mary

1958

A. M. D.

The Five First Saturdays and Reparation to the Immaculate Heart of Mary

1958

Nihil obstat

Leiria — 15 de Agosto de 1958.

CÓNEGO JOSÉ GALAMBA DE OLIVEIRA

Imprimatur

Leiren. 15 Augusti. 1958.

† JOANNES, VICARIUS CAPITULARIS

OFICINAS DA GRÁFICA DE LEIRIA

DEDICATION

Very humbly this little work is offered to the Sorrowful
and Immaculate Heart of the Queen of Heaven,
OUR MOTHER, in REPARATION

by

L. F. HARVEY Ter: O. S. M.

Servita of Fatima.

M. A. Oxon.

FÁTIMA.

The Feast of the Queenship of Mary.

1958.

FOREWORD

When one thinks of the very grave evils that threaten humanity ; and when one considers how many souls are lost and fall, every day, into the Abyss of Hell; and when one remembers that, in order to avoid those disasters and to save sinners, «God wants to establish in the world Devotion to My Immaculate Heart», *as Our Lady said when She appeared to the Three Little Shepherds of Fátima in July, Our heart rejoices at the appearance of one more little book that wishes to be a herald of that saving Devotion, and of the Five First Saturdays.*

May this little book run throughout the entire world, and may the Immaculate Heart of Mary bless, with Motherly liberality, its Author as well as all those who read it and put the Devotion into practice !

FÁTIMA, 13 de Junho de 1958.

† JOÃO, BISPO DE EURÉA
VIGÁRIO CAPITULAR

The Five First Saturdays and Reparation to the Immaculate Heart

«Oh Jesus, it is for love of You, for the conversion of sinners, and in Reparation to the Immaculate Heart of Mary!»

REQUEST FOR REPARATION

On July 13.1917, when the Holy Mother of God appeared to the Three Little Shepherds of Aljustrel, at the Cova da Iria in the Parish of Fatima, She spoke the words quoted above.

After promising to work a great Miracle in October, in order that «The whole world may believe you», and after demanding the Family Rosary, as well as the Daily Rosary, Our Lady said «Sacrifice yourselves for sinners, and say often, especially when you make sacrifices, 'Oh Jesus, it is for love of You, for the conversion of sinners, and in reparation for the offenses committed against the Immaculate Heart of Mary!'»

In the Autumn of 1916, the Guardian Angel of Portugal, who is held to be the Archangel Michael, and who came to prepare the three children for the coming of Our Lady with Her world-shaking Message in 1917, also demanded Reparation from the children, and through the children, from all of us!

Three times the Angel made the children, on the hill of Cabeço, repeat the following prayer before he gave them the Mystic Communion; He also made them say it, with him, again three times after receiving the Communion.

«Most Holy Trinity, Father, Son, and Holy Ghost I adore You profoundly, and I offer You the Most Precious Body and Blood, Soul and Divinity of Our Lord Jesus Christ, present in all the Tabernacles of the World, in reparation for all the outrages by which He Himself is offended. By the Infinite Merits of His Most Sacred Heart, and through the intercession of the Immaculate Heart of Mary, I pray for the conversion of all poor sinners!»

REPARATION TO GOD!

REPARATION TO OUR LADY!

Our God is a terrible God! «It is a fearful thing to fall into the Hands of the Living God!». Yet Our God is the God of Infinite Mercy and Infinite Love! God's Mercy is always the same, and when men repent and amend their lives He always forgives and spares! «Their pride is humbled. I will spare them from ruin.» 11 Para: XI. 7.

Why are we on Earth? Why are we alive? What is the point of our being here, on Earth, at all?

Simply to prepare for Heaven! Simply to give glory to God, to know and love and serve God here, in order that we may all be with Him in Heaven for ever!

There is no other reason for our existence!

We are simply and solely here on Earth for a time of TRIAL, in order to prepare ourselves for ETERNITY!

That Eternity will be for each of us simply and solely what we make it here, NOW!

That Eternity, which means a never-ending time, will be an Eternity of everlasting HAPPINESS, with the God of all Love, and with the Mother of Fair Love, and with all the Saints, boys and girls, men and women, and with all the Angels, in the endless enjoyment of such glorious surroundings as «Eye hath not seen, nor ear heard, nor has it entered into the heart of man», which God has there, in Heaven, waiting for those who accept His Holy Will! For those, who accept Him as their God and their King!

This joy is in store only for those who get to Heaven!

That Eternity, on the other hand, for which we are all now making preparation here on Earth, will be an ETERNITY, or never-ending time, of the most appalling, hateful, hideous, and unspeakable SUFFERING in the burning horrors of the endless TORTURE-CHAMBERS of HELL. That Eternity will be spent in the endless and nauseating company of the Hating and Hateful Devils in Hell, devils who are the slaves of Lucifer, and who with him were glorious Angels once, in the Heaven, which they have lost!

WHICH IS IT GOING TO BE FOR EACH OF US? WHICH IS IT GOING TO BE FOR ME? HEAVEN OR HELL?

It all depends on what I am doing about it now, or what I am going to do about it, before it is too late. «As the tree falls, so shall it lie!»

Almighty God, Himself, came down to Earth almost 2000 years ago, to win Heaven for us, to teach us how to get there, and to give us all the means that are necessary to get there.

Our Lady, Herself, has come to Earth many times and especially during the past 150 years, to warn us that we are heading for Hell, and to plead with us to OBEY Her Divine Son, to MAKE REPARATION for all the past sins of mankind, and TO AMEND OUR LIVES for the future.

These are the conditions for getting to Heaven!

God CANNOT MAKE us go to Heaven! Our Lady CANNOT MAKE us go to Heaven!

They are utterly incapable of doing that now, even with all God's almighty power!

The reason for this is that God gave to man FREE-WILL, and never, now, can He compel us to love Him! The choice has got to be made by each one of us!

The choice is — Shall I go the Heaven? OR Shall I go to Hell? Which shall it be?

THE ANSWER DEPENDS ENTIRELY UPON MY-SELF!

The answer to that question depends entirely upon ourselves! The choice is simply — Shall I go to Heaven? or, Shall I go to Hell?

IT ALL DEPENDS ON ME, MYSELF, HERE AND NOW!

GOD'S LOVE

Our God, Who is the God of INFINITE LOVE AND MERCY, Who loves each one of us with an unimaginable, unfathomable ocean of limitless love, came down to Earth to live as a poor working-man, and to die the death of a criminal, in order to SAVE US FROM ETERNAL HELL!

He came to take us to HEAVEN; thus repairing the terrible work of Adam and Eve.

Our Creator humbled Himself—simply out of love for each one us, for my sinful self—and was born in a wretched cattleshed! Just think of that! Just think of that unimaginable HUMILITY on the part of Almighty God!

The FIRST BED that God had, God Who made the Heavens and the Earth and every living thing, and every lifeless thing, that ever was or ever will be created, was a CATTLE-TROUGH, and His bedclothes were straw and hay! And the only beds that Mary and Joseph had, then, were piles of straw!

That was God Almighty's FIRST BED on Earth, that was the «gracious, kindly welcome» that mankind gave to Him in return for His immensity of love in coming to save us from THE ETERNITY OF HELL!

«Blow, blow thou wintry wind thou art not so unkind as man's INGRATITUDE!»

That, then, was the FIRST BED that God's «grateful» creatures made for Him.

And what was the LAST BED, allowed to Him by the same «grateful» creatures?

God's LAST BED on Earth was the HARD AND CRUEL, ROUGH AND AGONIZING CROSS.

We gave Him the CROSS, which was usually the last resting place of the vilest and worst CRIMINAL in existence, coupled with a death made as utterly cruel and painful as the science of the time could invent!

This was the extent to which the love of God for our souls went, and in the last moments of that agonizing death for love of man, God gave to us His greatest gift, after the gift of His own Self!

In those last painful hours, so empty of thought for Self, so full of love for us, the Dying Saviour gave to us HIS SPOTLESS MOTHER, to be OUR MOTHER!

The last word that the God-Man ever said to man, on Earth, before He died was—«MOTHER». BEHOLD THY MOTHER!

As God loved, and still does love, us, so in the same way Our Mother, in spite of all our cruelty to Her Baby and Her God, loves each one of us, singly, with all the love that there could be in the heart of one mother, if that mother had in her heart all the love of all the mothers in the whole world, as St Louis Grignon de Montfort teaches us.

This death, then, was just a part of the price that God paid for the redemption of our ungrateful souls, in order that we might go to Heaven, and be saved from Eternal Hell.

This Birth and Death was part of HIS price, as our Redeemer. Then there was the part of HER price, as our Co-Redemptrix.

All the indescribable sufferings endured in Bethlehem, and all those endured throughout Her whole long life, with those that She endured at the foot of the Cross, and when She held that dear mangled Body in Her loving Mother-arms, all those were a part of the price which SHE paid, as our Co-Redemptrix, for the saving of the souls of each one of us!

And all that would have been suffered for EACH ONE of us ALONE! Such an immense value does Our God set upon one single soul!

THE ARMS OF MERCY

Little Baby Jesus, lying there in the straw in the Stable of Bethlehem could, with His little Hands, touch the Dear Hands and the Sweet Face of His Blessed

Mother; He could touch the loving devoted, strong and faithful hands of St. Joseph, both of whom were His most faithful servants and protectors. Yes, those Baby arms stretched out in His little manger to embrace the whole wandering, wicked world, could also touch the soft skin of those two dumb animals, the Cow and the Donkey; He could lay His little Hand upon their heads to thank them for their kindness in allowing Him to share their stall, when men had turned Him out, and for warming Him with their hot breath.

Oh, fortunate beasts, so much more charitable, and so much more faithful, than so many of us have been to our loving Jesus!

There, in that little cattle trough, in the cold and draughty stable, cast out like any unwanted outcast, the Little Jesus lay at the beginning of His suffering life. Little Jesus lay there opening wide His Baby Arms to every soul, longing to fold them all close to His Baby Heart to keep them from all evil, to hold them all safely until they have arrived unharmed in His Father's home, there to spend a life of everlasting happiness, real happiness, with Him in Heaven.

That is how His blessed life began on Earth—Arms, Baby Arms, stretched out in longing love; Little Arms that He could wave at will!

Then how did that same life come to its end, on Earth?

It came to an end just in the same way, as far as the Arms were concerned! Arms, full grown, strong, loving Arms opened wide and stretched out to their fullest limit to embrace all sinners, to fold every soul in a loving, forgiving and eternal embrace, close to that Sacred Heart, which at that moment was giving the very last drops of His Most Precious Blood to save all men from Hell!

As those dear Arms were stretched out, wide open, in the cold and lonely Stable with the beasts, at the beginning of God's earthly life so now, at the end of it, those same dear Arms are stretched out wide on Calvary. This time, however, those dear Arms have been stretched out by others, and have been nailed fast to the cruel wood, so that now those once-Baby Arms cannot wave at will!

The beasts were round His bed in Bethlehem; kind friendly animals, who warmed Him with their hot breath. This time other «Beasts» are round Him, breathing hot hate against the God of Love! «Beasts» indeed, because all men who set themselves up against God, and sin against Him, make themselves «Beasts», or rather make themselves lower than all the beasts of the field!

You and I, WE were among those «Beasts» on Calvary! WE put the Son of God to death! We were among those Murderers! Because each sin that each of us has committed has «crucified the Son of God afresh»!

And for this each one of us is bound to MAKE REPARATION !

REPARATION

We, all of us, are bound to make Reparation, and that implies something ACTIVE, something DONE BY US. It is not, in any way, enough to FEEL SORRY and then do nothing at all about it, that is false sentiment. «Faith without works is dead!». The devils believe in God, but that belief is not enough to keep them from everlasting and hideous sufferings in Hell.

We, therefore, are bound to make REPARATION, and that being so let us all make sure that we know what Reparation means.

REPARATION simply means MAKING REPAIRS, repairing the damage and putting things right again, as far as we are able, doing all we can to MAKE IT UP.

Ever since the Fall of Man in the Garden of Eden, there has been a demand for Reparation. The Prophets of the Old Testament repeatedly demanded Reparation, and cried out unceasingly—«Repent! Repent!» Then came the last and greatest prophet of them all, according to the witness of Our Lord Himself, the great Prophet St. John the Baptist who spent a life of Reparation during which he cried out, again, and again, «Repent! For the Kingdom of Heaven is at hand!» as he prepared the way for the Lamb of God.

After St. John, came Jesus Himself crying out to all — «Unless ye repent, ye shall all likewise perish!»

And what does 'Repent' mean except, 'change your way of life', show your sorrow for your past sins and your past life by living a better life, by MAKING-UP for your past life, that is by making REPARATION!

Our tender - hearted, ever - merciful Saviour, the God of Compassionate Love, never minced His words; though He loved, and always loves, the SINNER, He hates with an all-consuming hatred, such as God alone can conceive, every SIN and all PRIDE, which is the root of all sin!

He, the All- Holy God, has bolted and barred the gates of Heaven against every one of us, UNLESS WE BECOME LIKE LITTLE CHILDREN — «Nisi efficiamini sicut parvuli». «Unless you become like little children you shall not enter into the Kingdom of Heaven». How heart-searching that is for us! Am I child-like? *Child-like* that is, not childish!

Or am I conceited, stuck-up, proud, and selfish? If I am, then I have not the slightest hope at all of going to Heaven—UNLESS I CHANGE ! Unless I become like a little child, humble, trusting and obedient !

«Like little children !»

When little children come into this world to begin their young, and happy, and hopeful lives they are so simple, so loving, so completely trusting, and so forgiving. This is how they come and remain, UNTIL they are ruined by the evil example or by the CRUEL SPOILING AND PAMPERING of parents, or others around them, all of which turns these little, loving innocents into odious, obnoxious and dangerous members of Society !

Before such spoiling happens, and that spoiling can often begin in the cradle itself, little children are so loving, so forgiving, so full of loving Reparation ! (There is an old saying — «The hand that rocks the cradle rules the world», which might, with profit today, be turned into «The hand which RULES the cradle, rocks the world!»)

Who cannot remember seeing a little child, when it has done something that hurt its mother, or when someone else has done something to hurt its mother, run to its mother, cuddle up to her, leaning its little head on her face or breast and try to comfort her ? «Oh, Mummy darling, I am so sorry, I love you, I really do and I am going to kiss you to MAKE IT UP !» Then by way of making Reparation, the little one gives her something, «Here, take my toy !».

«Like little children !» And all that God asks us to do, is to do the same.

«Oh, my Jesus, I am so sorry! I love You! I really do love You, and I am going to give You this, to do this for You, TO MAKE IT UP !»

«Oh, dearest Mother, I am so sorry! I love You! I really do love You, and I am going to give You this, to do this for You, to MAKE IT UP !

Yes, first the Prophets, then Jesus Himself, and now Our Lady, Herself, all demand Reparation !

Jesus demands REPARATION, Our Lady demands REPARATION.

The main purpose of this little book is to lay all possible stress upon, and to make an appeal to souls, to all souls, to make, THE REPARATION DEMANDED by OUR LADY AT FATIMA, with more especial emphasis on the Reparation of the FIVE FIRST SATURDAYS; and to do this before it is too late !

«PLORANS PLORAVIT IN NOCTE ET LACHRIMÆ EJUS IN MAXILLIS EJUS»
(Lam. 1, 2)

«Weeping, She hath wept in the night, and Her tears are on Her cheeks».

The oceans of iniquity in the world of today, and of yesterday, have brought oceans of tears into the Eyes of the God-Man, Our Lord Jesus Christ, and into the eyes of the Mother of Sorrows, Our Lady, the Mother of Jesus.

Knowing the most terrible sufferings that were soon to come upon the people, and seeing the number of people falling into Hell through neglect of His warnings, Jesus looked over Jerusalem, His own chosen city, and He broke down and wept !

Hot, burning tears of agonizing grief swept down His Face, the most beautiful Face that ever was seen in this world of ours.

«JESUS WEPT ! The Heart of God broke with sorrow for us! «If ONLY you had known, and that in this your day, the things that are to your PEACE !» «If only you had known, before it was TOO LATE !» He says to us today! This He says to us, today, in 1958, to us who long for peace and who make all kinds of plans for peace, instead of using His OWN PLAN, which was made known to us by Our Lady at Fatima!

Not very long after these burning tears were streaming down His Sacred Face, Jesus was on His way to the horrifying death of the Cross.

On His way to that terrible suffering Jesus passed some of the women of Jerusalem, the very ones whose fate had caused Him to weep sometime before.

What did Jesus say to those women?

«Don't weep for Me!» «Weep for YOURSELVES!» «Weep for YOUR CHILDREN!»

You see He knew what was coming to them, and to us!

JESUS WEPT! and MARY WEEPS!

Let us consider some of the visits, which Our Lady has made to this world within the last Century and a quarter. Let us see how often She appeared SAD, and how frequently She WEPT! And let us remember that She came to warn us, and the tears were because of the terrible sufferings to come upon us, which we could have avoided, and still can avoid, if only we had, or will, pay attention to Her warnings and requests.

At La Salette, in France in 1846, Our Lady appeared to some children and complained bitterly of the carelessness and sinfulness of the Catholics. She demanded Penance and Prayer, She demanded REPARATION, in order that we might be spared the terrible punishments of God, which are to come upon us if we do not OBEY HER.

All the time that Our Lady was speaking, SHE WAS CRYING, tears were pouring down Her face, the most beautiful face in all creation, next to that of Her own Divine Son.

Later, again, in 1858, Our Lady came once more to warn us and to demand the same REPARATION.

This time it was again in France, that «Elder daughter of the Church», which has so often been visited by, and honoured by, the Heavenly Queen. This time it was at Lourdes, in the Mountains in the South of France.

Eighteen times Our Lady spoke to little Bernadette, demanding PENANCE, HUMILITY, AND the RO-SARY OF REPARATION.

Our Lady's warnings were terrible; Her grief for the sinful world was tremendous !

A third time in France, in 1871, Our Lady came again, during the War between France and Germany, and again She spoke to children in a little, then unknown, place named Pontmain.

See how often Our Lady has chosen LITTLE CHIL-DREN to be Her Messengers, and to spread in the world Her tremendous messages! «Unless you become like little children you shall not enter into the Kingdom of Heaven !»

This time, when speaking, Our Lady was «INEFFA-BLY SAD», — during a part of the interview, and She held a Blood Red Crucifix.

Again and again Our Mother comes to save us from the wrath of God, Whose avenging Arm, She says, She «cannot longer withold!»; It is «so strong, so heavy».

Still She comes to call us to our senses! Still Our Mother weeps!

Still She shows us Her Immaculate Heart!

Once again Our Lady came, riding upon the clouds, surrounded by a cloud, and speeding down to Earth to warn us that the terrible results of our sins and of our neglect of God, were about to fall upon us more heavily than ever, in the form of Diabolic, Anti-God Communism.

Our Lady came to Fatima just about one month before that flood of bestial cruelty, more bestial than that of the cruellest of all the savage beasts themselves, that ocean of hate against the God of Love, burst in over-whelming torrents upon the world!

The Holy Mother came in the middle of the scourge of the 2nd World-War, a war in which millions of bodies and houses were being destroyed, millions of homes were being broken, millions of souls were being destroyed, a war in which children and grown-ups were being taught to hate their neighbour, together with all the paralysing evils that always accompany wars, especially modern wars! In the midst of all this, Our Lady PROMISED PEACE, that peace for which the whole world is still longing, if we FULFILLED the CONDITIONS, which She then laid down.

The world did not, and has not, fulfilled the conditions, and so the world has been reduced to the condition in which it finds itself today!

Our Lady demanded REPARATION, and by way of doing this She demanded that we should all do our DUTY to GOD, and our DUTY to our NEIGHBOUR- *as well as we can;* added to this Our Lady demanded that we should all accept whatever God may choose to send us, or, allow us to suffer, in this life, by way of PENANCE.

In addition, God's Mother, and Our Mother, told us to say the ROSARY EVERY DAY; and, thirdly, told us that we must all be CONSECRATED TO HER IMMACULATE HEART.

That is the ESSENCE of the MESSAGE OF FATIMA. During the last Apparitions, on October 13. 1917, Our Lady showed Herself as

THE MOTHER OF SORROWS

the Mother, Who was swamped in an ocean of suffering all through Her life. The Mother of Sorrows, Whose pains were caused by the sins of the world, by OUR private SINS.

The appearances of Our Lady at Fatima, in 1917, were some of the greatest and the most important in the whole history of the world!

THE SADNESS OF THE IMMACULATE HEART

Soon Our Lady came again to warn us, this time it was at Beauraing, in Belgium, in 1932. Here, again, Our Lady spoke to children and, as at La Salette, golden rays were shining round Her Heart. Golden rays of HOPE, for it is through that same Immaculate Heart that this world is to find PEACE, because it was revealed to little Jacinta of Fatima that God will give peace to the World THROUGH THE IMMACULATE HEART OF MARY.

At Fatima Our Lady showed Her Heart surrounded with thorns which, She said, represented our sins and our blasphemies; and She insisted that love for HER IMMACULATE HEART MUST be spread throughout the world, in order to obtain the destruction of the Devil's work and for the eventual triumph of right.

«My IMMACULATE HEART» She said, «WILL FINALLY TRIUMPH».

When Lucy, the eldest of the Seers of Fatima who is now a Carmelite Nun, asked Our Lady if the other two AND herself would soon go to Heaven, Our Lady answered that the other two would soon go, but that Lucy would not go yet, because God wanted her to stay on earth, in order to SPREAD THROUGHOUT THE WORLD LOVE FOR HER IMMACULATE HEART.

That is the immense vocation given to Lucy, and that ought to be a work, which each one of us should do with all our power, BECAUSE IT IS OUR LADY'S WISH, and what Our Lady wishes should be binding upon Her Children.

«If you love Me, keep My commandments!» That is the sign, and the proof of our love! If we do not do what the Loved one tells us then we DO NOT LOVE Him, or, Her, however much we may say, or sing, that we do !

Still more recently Our Lady of the Immaculate Heart has shown Her grief, in the little Statue, at Syracuse, which shed what appeared to be human tears. This has been authenticated also, and a huge Church is to be built.

These visits are enough to show the immense importance that Our Lord, and consequently Our Lady, places upon the NECESSITY of IMMEDIATE REPARATION.

We know that Our Lady can no longer suffer in Heaven, but She knows that we are only human, and She gives us visions that we can understand, and which can touch our hearts, unless they have become like stone or ice, through our neglect of God and all Spiritual things.

Time after time Our Lady has shown Herself in recent years, and has tried to make us feel some tiny bit of the unspeakable grief and sorrow that Her Divine Son and Herself felt on Earth all through Their lives, and especially during the Passion and Death of Our Lord.

Grief, this was, which was caused by the knowledge

of all the sins, and coldness and hatred, which we in the world should give Them in return for that Sea of Suffering !

Let us remember the untold Sorrows of the Queen of Sorrows, the Queen of Martyrs, when She was on Earth ! Let us remember the many times that Our Loving Mother has shown us tears and sadness in very recent visions !

Then let us DETERMINE, here and now, to give ourselves up to a LIFE OF REPARATION !

No ! This is not frightening ! This will be VERY SIMPLE AND VERY EASY, IF only we will do as She has asked and if we rely on Her and ACCEPT HER HELP !

St Louis Grignon de Montfort, that great and simple lover of Our Lady, tells us that if we will only give ourselves to Her, She will so soften our Crosses that they will become much more easy to bear.

IF THE WORLD DOES NOT LISTEN VERY SOON, THEN THE FUTURE SUFFERINGS, WHICH ARE COMING UPON US, ARE TOO UTTERLY FRIGHTENING TO THINK ABOUT !

It is the Mother of Divine Wisdom, no less than that, Who has warned us !

A TONIC AND A REMINDER

«What the eye does not see, the heart does not grieve over !» «Out of sight out of mind !»

Here are two old sayings, which apply very fittingly to a vast number of people in the world today.

The love of so many for God and the things of God has grown so terribly, terribly COLD, to a great extent through the pleasure-loving materialism of our day.

It is part of the policy of the Devil and his followers to encourage this blind foolishness on the part of his victims. So many victims are walking straight to the scaffold, of their own making, with their eyes blindfolded!

If people are always occupied with their own personal affairs, with their pleasures, with sport and entertainment, and the like, they are not going to be bothered about what is happening in the background, or what overwhelming dangers overhang their lives, and threaten the very occupations that they are so busily engaged in! They feel that the present occupations are «sufficient for the day», foolish and selfish argument though it may be !

This attitude suits the Devil and his friends absolutely, because they have their future victims mesmorised into a state in which they can be more easily destroyed — in which in fact they can destroy themselves. Those who have eyes open have seen this in recent history.

This is what is happening, now, in the middle of the 20th Century, and it needs an immense shock to rouse people out of their lethargy.

For years now Our Lady has been trying to rouse us into saving action, and at Fatima, at least, She worked one world-shaking Miracle, when She hurled the Sun towards the Earth, and petrified with fear, not only the 70,000 people on the spot, who saw it in the Cova da Iria, but many other people also, who saw that Miracle, miles and miles away !

That shock brought many souls to their knees, to their senses and to their Confessions, but—«What the eye does not see the heart does not grieve over», and the majority of the people in the world did not see that frightening event and consequently did not, and do not, grieve.

Nevertheless many millions of people have suffered, and are suffering now, from the neglect of that warning, and if only we could bring ourselves to realise but a tiny fraction of their sufferings, then it might, by the grace of God, give us that shock, which we so desperately need !

Let us go, at least in thought, to the very numerous Concentration Camps in Communist countries, where millions of people of all ages and ranks of society are dying a slow and painful death.

Let us talk to anyone, who has escaped from any part of the Red Hell!

Let us read the books that have been written by THOSE WHO KNOW, such as «I chose Freedom».

Let us read authentic accounts of the terrible Torture - chambers, of the Lubianko Prison, in Moscow, and of many others in other places !

Let us read about the millions of homeless CHILDREN, wandering like packs of wolves, covered with Venereal diseases, such as we read about in the early days of Russian Communism, in Russia itself—against which Our Lady came to warn us !

Let us read of the starving women fighting for the horse manure in the streets to pick out the grains of corn, which the horses had not digested, to help to keep those same women from dying of starvation !

Let us remember the endless number of people, who have disappeared suddenly, in the night as well as at other times, and who have never been heard of again!

Let us think of the hideous horrors of the two World Wars !

Let us think of the 1000's of prisoners, captured by the Russians in the last great war, who just «Disappeared»! Of those buried alive, or torn in pieces.

Many, many more terrible things could be said, unfortunately, but perhaps with the grace of God these horrors will be enough to make men, and women, stop and think — and then act !

There will be many, very many people, who will scoff, and jeer, and sneer at all this, and will say — «What absolute nonsense ! The man's a fool, who talks like that ! He is just an alarmist !»

Nay, listen ! «A fool is ever right in his own thinking; the wise LISTEN to advice !» Proverbs. XII. 15.

The fool is the one who says «There is no God !»

The fool is the one, who refuses to be warned by incontrovertible facts !

The fool is the one who throws away the lifebelt when he is drowning !

The fool is the one, who will not listen to the warnings of God and His Holy Mother, when They demand REPARATION !

These are the real fools !

«Oh, ye fools, when will you understand !»

For those who live far away from the countries where these unspeakable brutalities take place, and for those who cannot imagine that such diabolic cruelty can exist in the hearts of human beings, it must be very difficult to grasp the truth.

For those, however, who have come into direct contact with some of those human wrecks, who have been able escape from that inhuman, diabolic treatment received in those countries where the inhuman, Anti-Christian, Anti-God, Atheistic Materialism of Communism, and its satanic brood, hold power—for them it is easy to grasp something of the TERROR.

Those, who have come across the hunted, frightened Refugees from that infernal Hell, can feel *something* of the terror and the diabolic power, which only God and His Most Holy Mother can save us, and our dear loved ones, from experiencing and suffering also !

Oh, dear Outcast God, take care of the hunted, outcast people of today, and SPARE US ALL !

Oh, dear loving Mother, Who wast driven away by

men when Your time was drawing near, Who wast afterwards hunted by Herod, as You fled into Egypt, have pity on all homeless Waifs, and fold them to Your Immaculate Heart. Oh Dear Mother of the Infant Jesus have pity on the little children, and on the little babies, so grievously sinned against !

Oh ! God of Truth and Light and Wisdom and Understanding, open the eyes of all of us, who cannot— or will not — see the terrible disasters which lie ahead of all of us, unless we obey Our Lady and make REPARATION NOW !

THE REPARATION DEMANDED
BY OUR LADY

Since Our Lady came to Fatima, 41 years have passed; forty one years in which the Devil and all his hordes have been very busy trying to keep the Message of Fatima from being spread, and from being grasped, lest people should obey Our Lady and so save themselves, and help to save the world.

The Devil wants the damnation of souls — not their salvation !

For many, many years the Message of Fatima was never heard of, except by a few !

For many years there has been a fogginess, an uncertainty and a muddled idea of the real meaning of the Message.

Many of the devotees of Fatima have not even been clear themselves !

It is also well known by many, who have themselves experienced them, the great and typical difficulties, and dangers that are put in the way of people, who want to go to Fatima !

To those, who are willing to see, it is quite evident that the cloven hoof of the Prince of Darkness has been, and still is, fighting hard and fuming against Our Lady of Light !

We will now try to make Our Lady's demands quite clear, and show how SIMPLE they are.
One of the «Hallmarks» of Fatima is SIMPLICITY !

The demands of Our Lady

During the course of Her visits to Fatima, in 1917, Our Lady made

THREE DEMANDS

Three special demands were made upon the world, through the Three Little Shepherds of Aljustrel. Our Lady stated that only if a sufficient number of people obey these demands, the world will be saved from WAR, from the Horrors of COMMUNISM, and from the PUNISHMENTS OF GOD.
These three demands were:

PENANCE. PRAYER. CONSECRATION TO HER
IMMACULATE HEART.

PENANCE AND SACRIFICE are hard words to us, as well as being most unwelcome to most of us !
The word PENANCE makes us think of LONG FASTS, WHIPPING OURSELVES, WEARING HAIR SHIRTS, and doing all kinds of things that we thoroughly dislike.

THESE THINGS ARE NOT FOR US — NOR
DOES OUR LADY WISH THEM, FROM US

We are not expected to be like St John the Baptist,
and other great Saints and heroes in that way.

NO ! Ours is to be THE LITTLE WAY OF OBE-
DIENCE TO OUR LADY !

We are going to take these three demands of Our
Lady one by one, and we are going to see how simple
and easy they really are, if only we will try to be honest
with God and with ourselves.

During these explanations I shall quote from the
writings of Fr. de Marchi. I. M. C., who spent many
years in Fatima, and who knew the Marto family, as
well as Lucy and her family, very well.

I shall also quote from «Nossa Senhora da Fatima»,
in its third edition, by Fr. Fonseca. S. J., which is
acknowledged to be one of the most authentic and
most correct books on Fatima and its Message.

PENANCE AND SACRIFICE

«Whatsoever thine hand findeth to do, do it with
thy might !»

What is the Penance demanded from all of us by
Our Lady ?

In a letter, quoted by Fr. de Marchi, which Lucy
wrote to the Bishop of Leiria, we find the following
passage :

«... The Good Lord complains bitterly and sorrowfully
about the small number of souls in His grace, who are
willing to renounce whatever the observance of His
Law requires of them.

This is the penance, which the Good Lord now asks:

The Sacrifice that every person has to impose upon himself, is to lead a life of justice in the observance of His Law. He requires this way to be made known to souls. For many, thinking that the word 'Penance' means great austerities, and not feeling in themselves the strength, or the generosity, for these, lose heart and rest in a life of lukewarmness and sin.

Last Thursday, at midnight, while I was in the Chapel, with my Superior's permission, Our Lord said to me: — 'THE SACRIFICE REQUIRED OF EVERY PERSON IS THE FULFILMENT OF HIS DUTIES IN LIFE, AND THE OBSERVANCE OF MY LAW. THIS IS THE PENANCE THAT I NOW SEEK AND REQUIRE.'»

It is as simple as that! Here Our Lord confirms, and explains, the demand of Our Lady for SACRIFICE AND PENANCE!

IT IS SIMPLY THAT WE DO OUR DUTY TO GOD, AND TO OUR NEIGHBOUR AS WELL AS WE CAN

It is simply a demand that we should KEEP OUR BAPTISMAL PROMISES.

It is simply that we are to love God, and in loving God to avoid sin, and the occasions of sin, to set a good example — fearlessly — and be good Christians, with all that that implies.

THE SINS OF THE FLESH

Knowing the evil days in which we live, with all its immorality, its seductiveness, its immodesty and its bad influence on souls, Our Lady explained in detail to Jacinta many things, when she was in the house of

Mother Godinho, in Lisbon. Our Lady explained many things to this wonderful little girl, including some things dealing with impurities.

One thing, as Jacinta explained to Mother Godinho, was that «THE SINS WHICH BRING MOST SOULS TO HELL ARE THE SINS OF THE FLESH. CERTAIN FASHIONS OFFEND OUR LORD VERY MUCH. Those, who serve Our Lord, should not follow these fashions... People lose their souls, because they do not think about the Death of Our Lord, and DO NOT DO PENANCE.»

We need only think of the Advertisements in our countries, both in the streets and in the papers. We need only think of many of the Pictures, the Magazines, the Cinema, the Television, the Fashions, the Bathing dresses (?), the nakedness of the Naturalist colonies, the dirty jokes in conversations and books, the oceans of impurity in modern life, to realise that there is an immense opportunity, and necessity, for making sacrifices, sacrifices which are our plain duty to God and to our neighbour !

THESE sacrifices are a matter of DUTY.

There are other Sacrifices — VOLUNTARY SACRIFICES — which Our Lady asked for from the children, at Fatima, and though them from all generous souls.

Anyone, who loves deeply, will always find endless ways of making little sacrifices for the one they love!

Dearest Jesus, teach us to love Thee MORE, and give us a deeper love for Thy Holy Mother too !

When we make such Sacrifices Our Lady told us to say: — «Oh Jesus, it is for love of You, for the conversion of sinners, and in reparation to the Immaculate Heart of Mary!»

It is not so very hard to go without an occasional cigarette, or some other little pleasure; it is not so very difficult to go without a little drink sometimes when we are thirsty; or to keep back an unkind or hasty word, or criticism; it does not cost us much, and it ought not to cost us anything, to give up a few minutes to tell Our Lord, in the Tabernacle, that we love Him; it does not take so very long to say an extra Rosary!

There are many little ways of pleasing Our Lady, and making sacrifices, as the Three Little Shepherds of Fatima found out, and then acted so generously!

NEVERTHELESS THE ONLY SACRIFICE BIND-ING ON US, IS TO DO OUR DUTY WELL!

PRAYER. THE ROSARY.

The second point is the prayer of the Rosary.

Prayer is the lifting up of our hearts and minds to God. The greatest and most powerful, and most acceptable prayer in the sight of God, is the MASS.

The Mass is included in our duty to God, and we are bound to hear Mass on every Sunday and day of Obligation. That is understood.

Next to the Mass comes, for us, the Rosary. In Her visitations during recent years Our Lady has insisted upon the SAYING OF THE ROSARY. Our Lady knows the incalculable power of the Rosary, which is greater than all Atomic and other Bombs!

These lines are being written at the beginning of the Centenary Year of Lourdes, where the Holy Mother demanded the Rosary, where She taught little Berna, dette how to make the sign of the Cross reverently-and well, before saying the Rosary. Our Lady, Herself, said the Rosary with Bernadette.

NOBODY, on earth, KNOWS the unspeakable and incalculable POWER OF THE ROSARY.

The Devil knows it and he HATES it, hating the very thought of people saying the Rosary!

That being so, there is hardly any need of further argument to persuade people, who love God and Our Lady, as well as themselves, to say the Rosary very, very often !

At Fatima, and the Message of Fatima is essentially the weapon against the modern worldwide, soul destroying disease of Atheistic Communism and International Wars, Our Lady insisted, visit after visit, that we should say the Rosary EVERY DAY, and that we should say the FAMILY ROSARY also.

Let us also remember how often recent Popes, who are God's Representatives on Earth, have urged the saying of the Rosary. Let us remember the great victory of the Christians at the Battle of Lepanto, and other great triumphs, due to the saying of the Rosary!

At Fatima, as at Lourdes, Our Lady always appeared with a Rosary. When Lucy asked if Francisco would go to Heaven, Our Lady said that he would, but that he would have to say MANY ROSARIES first !

Before leaving the Cova da Iria on May 13, 1917., Our Lady said: — «Say the Rosary every day, with devotion, in order to obtain peace for the world!»

DO WE REALLY WANT PEACE? — the powers of evil do not want peace — If we do, then we must say the Rosary !

That is one of the essential conditions for Peace, laid down by God, through the Mediatrix of all the Graces!

On October 13, 1917, at Fatima the day of Her last appearance, Our Lady said that She was THE LADY OF THE ROSARY, and that we must always continue to say the Rosary EVERY DAY !

Therefore everyone of us is bound to say the Rosary every day.

By doing this we shall not only bring about the Conversion of Russia, and bring peace to the world, but we shall bring down untold blessings on the world and the people in it, we shall «conquer our enemies, check our passions, advance in virtue», and after we have crowned Our Lady with many «roses» on Earth we shall «go to see Her crowned with honour and glory in Heaven.»

THE FAMILY ROSARY

On July 13, 1917, at Fatima, when Lucy asked Our Lady to cure the little crippled boy, John Carreira, (who now looks after the Capelinha), Our Lady refused to cure him but said that he must say the Rosary EVERY DAY WITH HIS FAMILY.

THE FAMILY IS THE FOUNDATION
OF THE STATE

The FAMILY is the strength of the Church and of the Nation. The FAMILY is the first object of attack on the part of the Devil and the Communists.

If they can break up the HOME, and get at the CHILDREN, then they are well on the way to winning all the rest !

Our homes are in vital danger today. The destroying maggot is in our homes today, and it comes in with the consent of countless PARENTS. The destroying worm comes through many of the Papers, allowed into the homes, papers and magazines that would foul a manure heap, but which our children are allowed to absorb! The worm comes in through the UNCEN-

SORED use of the WIRELESS AND TELEVISION, through the lack of discipline and control, through the lack of HOME LOVE!

Childrens souls, today, are being sold for a MESS, not of potage as in the case of Esau, but for a MESS OF DIABOLIC AND IMMORAL PLEASURE!

Our Lady has given us a sure and certain remedy to save our homes, and that is

TO SAY THE FAMILY ROSARY EVERY DAY. «Because Our Lady wishes it.» (Lucy)

If we do not make the effort, and if thereby our homes are ruined and our children damned, there will be nobody to blame but ourselves!

And if we meet God, just after we die, and He says to us — «Go ye cursed into everlasting fire, prepared for the Devil and his angels!» we can blame noone but ourselves, because He told us that it would have been better for us to have been thrown over a cliff, with some stones round our necks, rather than that we should have caused scandal to one little child — and, God have mercy on us, many of us are doing that now!

One more very important thing!

On July 13, 1917, Our Lady told the children to say a little prayer

AFTER EACH DECADE OF THE ROSARY

This is done at Fatima, always, and in many another place, though many people have not yet learned to obey Our Lady, in this matter also. It is amazing that, in spite of all the warnings and in spite of all the amazing promises of wonderful blessings, 41 long years have passed and still people, people who know about Fatima, and pride themselves on it, simply ignore so much of what Our Lady asked us to do!

The prayer, which Our Lady told us to say after each decade of the Rosary is —

Oh, JESUS, FORGIVE US OUR SINS, SAVE US FROM THE FIRES OF HELL, AND LEAD ALL SOULS TO HEAVEN, ESPECIALLY THOSE MOST IN NEED OF THY MERCY!

Our Lord said — «If you love Me, keep My commandments!»

Little Jacinta of Fatima was inspired to say, about the appearances and revelations of Our Lady: — «If you dont want to believe, then you must expect the punishments of God.»

CONSECRATION TO THE IMMACULATE HEART OF MARY

This is the third demand of Our Lady, and it is VERY, VERY important.

For nine long months the Baby Heart of the Infant Jesus beat close to the Immaculate Heart of His Maiden Mother. Two Hearts, literally, beating as One! Mary's blood poured through the unborn Heart of the Eternal God.

In the Temple, the aged Simeon told the Virgin-Mother that a SWORD of SORROW would pierce Her Heart.

On Calvary, the Spear of St Longinus pierced the Sacred Heart of Jesus, and made so big a hole that St Thomas could put his hand right into it! At the same moment a cruel sword of sorrow pierced the Immaculate Heart of His Mother, as She stood at the foot of the Cross! Two Hearts pierced, as One!

In recent Centuries, devotion to These Two Hearts, has been preached by many, notably by St John Eudes.

During the first half of our own century — though

the Church has not yet pronounced on this — many important revelations are claimed to have been received by Bertha Petit, in relation to the Sacred Hearts, all of which were known to Pope Benedict XV, to St Pius X. and to others.

WE have been redeemed by the Blood of Jesus, poured out for us in His Passion !

WE have been given Eternal Life, if we wish to receive it, through the Blood of Jesus!

The Human Body of Jesus was given life by the blood poured into It from the sinless Heart of His Mother, Mary! Her blood gave Him life!

How can we separate the Sacred Hearts?

In 1916, at Cabeço, near Fatima, the Angel had united the Sacred Hearts in his prayer, taught to the three children.

Our Lady Herself, at the very first appearance at Fatima, had asked for Reparation for the sins committed against the Divine Majesty (The Sacred Heart) and for the blasphemies against Her own Immaculate Heart.

It was revealed to little Jacinta that God wants the Immaculate Heart of His Mother to be honoured, *side by side*, with His own Sacred Heart.

In the second visit, at Fatima, Our Lady told Lucy that she would have to stay on Earth because God wanted her to make Our Lady «known and loved», «to establish in the world devotion to My Immaculate Heart», and Our Lady added — «I promise salvation to everyone, who will embrace that devotion; they will be the chosen souls of God, like flowers placed by Me before His throne!» When Lucy asked if she would have to stay on Earth all alone, Our Lady answered — «No, my child! Does it cause you much suffering? Dont be downhearted! I will never leave you! My Immaculate Heart will be your Refuge, and the Way that will lead you to God!»

What need is there of anything more? There is no need!

If we want to be protected in this world, if we want to go to Heaven for ever, then all we have to do is to cast ourselves into the Immaculate Heart of Mary, to give ourselves, and that means to CONSECRATE ourselves, to Her, to be ALL HERS FOR EVER!

By doing this we shall belong entirely to God, for what we give to Her, She gives to God! SHE IS THE WAY THAT WILL LEAD US TO GOD!

Our Lady asks for the CONSECRATION OF EVERYBODY, of RUSSIA, of the WHOLE WORLD, TO HER IMMACULATE HEART.

Our Lady said, at Fatima: — «My Immaculate Heart will finally triumph! So that it is through the Immaculate Heart... that PEACE is to COME to the world!

It is through the Immaculate Heart that souls are to be converted, and sinners are to be brought back to God!

It is through the Immaculate Heart that the TRIUMPH of God's CHURCH is to come!

It is quite clear where our duty lies; it lies in consecrating ourselves to the Immaculate Heart of Mary!

Here is a short Act of Consecration to the Immaculate Heart, which has the Imprimatur of the Diocese of Leiria (Fatima).

«Oh, DEAREST, PUREST MOTHER, OUR LADY OF FATIMA, I GIVE MYSELF TO YOU TO BE ALL YOURS FOR EVER! ALL THAT I AM AND ALL THAT I HAVE I GIVE TO YOU! PLEASE KEEP ME AS YOUR OWN!»

THE OUTWARD SIGN OF OUR CONSECRATION IS TO BE THE WEARING OF THE SCAPULAR!

THE FIVE FIRST SATURDAYS

Now we have one thing, and that a MOST IM-
PORTANT THING, left, which brings us to the climax
of this little work, and to the Title of our little book!

We have spent a long time in preparing for it, BE-
CAUSE IT IS VERY IMPORTANT!

We have been speaking of Reparation, which Our
Lady has so often demanded in recent years; and we
have tried to make quite clear, what She has asked for.

Our Lady has asked the World for —

REPARATION TO, AND THROUGH, HER IM-
MACULATE HEART

More than this, Our Lady has requested that this
Reparation shall take a special form, in union with
the Sacred Heart!

You see this is just what we have been saying — YOU
CANNOT SEPARATE THE SACRED HEARTS.

Our Lady asked for A COMMUNION OF REPA-
RATION ON THE FIRST SATURDAY OF EVERY
MONTH.

In this way we are making reparation to Both the
Sacred Hearts, and the Immaculate Heart is leading
us straight to the Sacred Heart of Jesus, three to find the
food and strength to nourish our souls, to give us the grace
to do our duty to God and man, to lead us closer to
God, and Our Lady, and to take us eventually to Heaven!

On July 13, 1917, Our Lady told the there children,
in the Cova da Iria that She was coming to «ask for
the consecration of Russia to My Immaculate Heart,
and THE COMMUNION OF REPARATION ON
THE FIRST SATURDAYS... If people attend to My
requests, Russia will be converted and there WILL BE
PEACE;...»

THERE WILL BE PEACE.

Have we yet a stable peace? Has Russia been converted to the Catholic Faith? God knows, and we know to our cost, that Russia has not been converted!

Many martyred Nations know that too! Millions of human slaves, of human wrecks know that too! Millions of little, broken homeless children and babies know that too! (God forgive us!) Many over burdened, heart-broken, semi-ruined tax-payers know that too!

And why is there all this hideous, unnecessary, suffering? Simply and solely because

WE HAVE NOT OBEYED OUR LADY!

Our Lady also asked us, in making our Communions on the first Saturdays of the month to make the

FIVE FIRST SATURDAYS

just in the same way as we make the Nine First Fridays. That is to say, we are to make the Five First Saturdays, *without a break*, doing three things.

The practice of the *Five First Saturdays* consist 1) in Making Our Confession and Communion. 2) In saying the Rosary devoutly. 3) In spending a Quarter of an hour, *in meditation*, on one or more of the 15 Mysteries of the Rosary, with the intention of making REPARATION!

Little Jacinta, the youngest of the three Seers of Fatima was a tower of strength to the others, and God gave her special lights to understand Our Lady's Message, baby girl though she was! After going to Hospital the little girl said to Lucy;—

«I am going to Heaven soon. You are going to stay on here to tell the people that God wants to establish in the world devotion to the Immaculate Heart of Mary. When you are going to tell them that, don't hide yourself.

Tell everybody that God gives us His graces through the Immaculate Heart of Mary; that they must ask for them through Her; that the Heart of Jesus wants to be honoured, side by side, with the Immaculate Heart of Mary; that they must ask for peace through the Immaculate Heart of Mary, because God has given it into Her keeping.»

Is not all this crystal clear? Our Lady is the Queen and Giver Of PEACE!

Our Lady left, the years passed by, Francisco and Jacinta went to Heaven, and Lucy became a Nun. Then one day, eight years later, on December 10, 1925, Our Lady appeared to Lucy once again, carrying in Her arms the Baby Jesus.

The Holy Mother showed Her Heart to Lucy, all surrounded with thorns. Then the Baby Jesus, pointing to the Suffering Heart of His Mother, said:—

«Have pity on this Heart, continually tormented by the ingratitude of men, with nobody to make Reparation!»

Oh, let us listen to, and answer, that Baby pleading! Who can refuse a baby's cry, especially when that Baby is Jesus, God of Love?

After the Infant Jesus had said this, Our Lady added:

«Look, My child, look at My Heart surrounded with thorns, with which ungrateful men pierce it, at every moment, by their blasphemies and ingratitude! Do you, at least, try to console Me; and tell everybody from Me that all, who on the First Saturday of Five consecutive months shall make their Confession and Communion, shall say the Rosary, and shall keep Me company for 15 minutes, while Meditating on the Rosary, with the intention of making Reparation, tell them from Me that I promise to help them, at the hour of their death, with all the graces necessary for the salvation of their souls.»!

Two months later, on February 15, 1926, Our Lady again appeared with the Holy Child and urged Lucy to persevere in propagating the devotion to Her Immaculate Heart, in spite of all difficulties.

Lucy asked Our Lady if it was sufficient to make the *Confession* «during the week», when it was not possible to make it on the First Saturday. Our Lady answered «Yes», provided that the Communion was received in a *state of grace, and* with the intention of making the *required Reparation.*

Oh! What goodness of Our Lady! Oh! What Mercy of Our God! Could anybody be so MAD as to refuse that safe offer of Salvation!

REMEMBER !

CONFESSION. THE ROSARY. 15 *MINUTES MEDITATION ON THE ROSARY:*

ALL WITH THE INTENTION OF *MAKING REPARATION*, ON 5 CONSECUTIVE SATURDAYS!

With this goes the promise of *Our Lady's help at death, and Eternal Life!*

BUT DONT FORGET, ALSO, A COMMUNION OF REPARATION ON EVERY FIRST SATURDAY!

Because Our Lady wishes it!

Is it not utterly inconceivable that now, 41 years after Our Lady made these requests and these staggering promises, so many, SO VERY MANY, catholics pay no attention to them?

Are we really so hard-hearted that we do not want

to save MILLIONS of people from a Hell of suffering, both here and hereafter?

Are we really so hard-hearted that we do not want PEACE for the world?

Are we really such senseless people that we do not want to make OUR HEAVEN CERTAIN?

No! No! Perhaps we have not known! Perhaps we have not thought! Perhaps, even, we have been misled by weak men, or by false prophets!

This little work, with all its faults and all its shortcomings, is written with a burning longing that all men should know Our Lady's wishes and should do their *utmost* to fulfil them! It is an attempt to bring right home to the hearts of all, especially of those who have not yet grasped them, Our Mother's pleadings and Our Mother's wishes, as She expressed them here on this very spot — this most holy ground!

Every single word, written here in the Cova da Iria, where Our Lady appeared just 41 years ago, is a pleading with the Holy Spirit, through the Immaculate Heart of His Most Holy Spouse, to come down upon this world in OCEANS and in CATARACTS of GRACE, to lead all men TO CONSECRATE themselves to the IMMACULATE HEART OF MARY, MOTHER OF THE ETERNAL GOD AND OUR MOTHER. It is a pleading, also, that — for their own salvation, for the salvation of others, for the Peace of the world, for the Honour and Glory of God, for the Honour of the Immaculate Heart of Mary — they will practice always the devotion of: —

THE FIVE FIRST SATURDAYS OF FIVE CONSE-CUTIVE MONTHS, in love of and reparation to THE IMMACULATE HEART OF MARY!

«Behold thy Mother!» «Unless you become as LITTLE

CHILDREN you shall NOT ENTER into the Kingdom of Heaven!»

What does a LITTLE CHILD do? A little child ALWAYS AND FIRST runs to its MOTHER, clings to its MOTHER, seeks the protection and help of its MOTHER, looks to its MOTHER for food and for everything else! Without its MOTHER a little child is lost !

Jesus has told us to look to our Mother and to act as little children do! Let us turn to Her, in Whom is «All the grace of the way and of truth» and all «hope of life»! Let us obey Him, by obeying Her! Then we shall be safe and we shall be saved!

«Tender arms of Mary, soft and warm and true,
«All my soul is yearning in the dark for You !»
(M. Kinder)

Praise be to God, to Our Lady, and to good St Joseph for another little work completed.

«Oh! Sorrowful and Immaculate Heart of Mary, pray for us who have recourse to Thee!» (300 days).

Made in the USA
Middletown, DE
29 February 2024

50482272R00027